To be the best,
you've got to
HIRE the best.

To hire the best,
you've got to
ATTRACT the best.

To attract the best,
you've got to
BE the best.

180 ways to build a

MAGNETIC CULTURE

Practical "How To's" For Retaining,
Attracting, and Hiring The Best, Brightest,
and Most Productive People

Eric Harvey
Mel Kleiman

To order additional copies of
180 Ways To Build A Magnetic Culture
or for information on other
WALK THE TALK® products and services,
contact us at
1.888.822.9255
or visit our website at
www.walkthetalk.com

The WALK THE TALK® Company

Printed in the United States of America
10 9 8 7 6 5 4 3 2

ISBN 1-885228-39-2

Edited by Jill Mason and Juli Baldwin
Printed by MultiAd

It's a fact! Our pool of qualified talent is quickly evaporating and relief is nowhere in sight.

Fast-forward a few short years and you'll find that as many as four million jobs go begging because of a lack of qualified candidates. Fast-forward ten years and the shortfall is projected to be at least 20 million – possibly as great as 30 million. Regardless of your function or level within your organization, one way or another, you will be affected!

What once was a seasonal skirmish for new workers has turned into a full-fledged, year-round war. Companies that used to go after their competitors' customers now chase after their competitors' best employees!

Today, every employer competes directly with every other employer for needed bodies and minds. But even in light of this battle for resources, there are many strategies that can help you minimize turnover and attract the talent you need. You'll find 180 of those strategies as you read on. And as you read, you'll need to pay close attention, because one of today's most pressing business challenges is building what we call a "magnetic culture" – one that naturally attracts and retains the best … and repels the rest.

Building such a culture requires values-driven practices, tough-minded hiring standards, and extraordinary levels of respect for the people you work with and those who work for you.

A&P • Abbott Labs • Ace Hardware • Alcoa • Allstate •
Amazon.com • AMD • America West Airlines • America
Airlines • American Express • American Standard •
Ameritech • Anheuser-Busch • Ann Taylor • Aramark •
Army & Air Force Exchange • Arthur Anderson • Ashlan
Chemical • AT&T • Bank of America • Barnes & Noble
• Baxter Healthcare • Bell South • Beneficial Savings •
Best Buy • BlueCross BlueShield • Boeing • BP-Amoco
Brinker International • Bristol Hotels • Bristol-Meyers
Squibb • Burlington Northern Santa Fe • Caesars Palace
• Caterpillar • Cendant • Centerior Energy • Cessna •
Chambersburg Hospital • Charles Schwab • Chase Bank
Cigna • Cisco Systems • City of Carrollton • City of Dalla
• Coca-Cola • Colgate- Palmolive • Comerica Bank •
CommuniCare • Compass Bank • ConnectCo • Consolidat
Stores • Consumer's Energy • The Container Store •
Continental Airlines • Con-Way • Cornell University •
Costco • DaimlerChrysler • Dana Corporation • Del Web
Corp. • Dell Computer • Delta Airlines • Detroit Edison
Disney • Domino's Pizza • Duke Power • DuPont • Eagle
Communications • EDS • Emerson Electric •
Equilon/Equiva • ExxonMobil • Fannie Mae • Federal
Express • Federal Reserve • Federated Department Stores
First Data Merchant Services • Footaction • Ford Motor
Company • Fortune Magazine • Franklin Covey • Gale
Group • GAP • Gateway • GE • General Motors • Georgi
Power • Gingiss International • Godiva • Growmark •
Harley-Davidson • Herman Miller • Hewlett Packard •
Hoechst • Home Depot • HON Industries • Hughes Aircra
Humana • Huntsman • Hyatt Hotels • Intel • Inventec
Electronics • Johnson Controls • Johnson & Johnson • J.
Morgan • Kaiser Hospitals • Kerr-McGee • KFC • Kimber
Clark • Kingsbury • K-Mart • Kraft Foods • LabCorp

This book is dedicated to our valued clients ...

Lafarge • Libbey-Owens Ford • Lockheed Martin • Loews
• Lucent Technologies • Marathon Oil • Marriott •
Martin Marietta • Maytag • McDonald's • Mellon Bank
• Memorial Health • Merck • Mercy Health Partners •
Meristar Hotels • Merrill Corp. • Merrill Lynch • Microsoft
Mohawk Industries • Motorola • NASA • National Park
Service • National Transit Institute • Nestle • New York
Times • Nextel Communications • Nike • Nordstrom •
Norfolk Public Schools • Nortel • Northern States Power •
Northwestern Mutual • Novartis • Ocean Spray • OfficeMax
Ortho-McNeil • Oshman's • OXY • PacMed • Panasonic •
PepsiCo • Pfizer • Phillip Morris • Pillsbury • Pitney Bowes
Pizza Hut • Playtex • Pratt & Whitney • Price Waterhouse

... organizations and leaders
who truly understand the importance
of building a Magnetic Culture.

Coopers • Procter & Gamble • Providence Health Systems •
Provident Bank • Prudential • PSE&G • Quaker Oats •
Queens Health Network • Ralston Purina • Red Roof Inns
• Safeway • Saks Fifth Avenue • SBC • Schlage Locks •
Schlumberger • S.C. Johnson and Son • Seagate • Sears •
ServiceMaster • Shaws • Shell • Snap-on Tools • Sodexho
Marriott • Southern Companies • Southern Ohio Medical
Center • Southwest Airlines • Spirit Energy • Sprint • St.
Charles Hospital • St. John's Hospital & Medical Center •
St. Vincent Hospital • Starbucks Coffee • Starwood • State
Farm • State of California • State of Kansas • Steelcase •
Sun Microsystems • Tenneco • Texas Health Resources •
GSLC • TIC Inc. • Time Warner • Transamerica • TRICON
TXU • Union Carbide • Union Pacific • United Healthcare
University of Oklahoma • University of Virginia • UPS •
USAA • U.S. Airways • U.S. Armed Forces • USF&G •
U.S. Postal Service • U.S. West • The Venetian Resort &
Casino • Verizon • Wal-Mart • Washington Hospital Center •
Waste Management • Wells Fargo • Westin Hotels • YMCA

mag·net·ic

(măg-net′ĭk) *adj.*

Of or relating to magnetism or magnets; having an unusual power or ability to attract.

cul·ture

(kŭl-chər) *n.*

The totality of socially transmitted behavior patterns, arts, beliefs, institutions, and all other products of human work and thought characteristic of a community or population.

The **3** Components of Building a
MAGNETIC CULTURE

> **R**ETENTION ... *Keep 'em*
>
> **A**TTRACTION ... *Find 'em*
>
> **S**ELECTION ... *Get 'em*

Magnetic Cultures are
SELF-PERPETUATING

Effective RETENTION strategies
shape environments that **attract** good
candidates to **select** from

RETENTION

SELECTION

Effective SELECTION
strategies bring on good
people who help you
retain and **attract** others

ATTRACTION

Effective ATTRACTION
strategies make it easier
to **select** good people to
retain

Contents

Getting Started

How to get the most from this handbook ...

First, read the handbook from cover to cover with a highlighter in hand. Mark any key words or phrases that you find particularly relevant and meaningful.

Next, select three ideas or action items that you wish to personally adopt. Circle the number of each item you select (1-180) and mark the pages they appear on with "sticky notes." Review those pages frequently.

Finally, each time you complete or master one of your action items, draw an "X" through its circled number and select a new item to work on in its place. That way, you'll have three ideas working at all times. Before you know it, your handbook will be filled with crossed-out numbers, and you'll be well on your way to building *your* Magnetic Culture.

retention

To attract and hire the best, you've got to BE the best

Building a Magnetic Culture begins with focusing on **retention** techniques. When it comes to people, there's little sense in trying to find 'em and get 'em if you haven't figured out how to *keep* 'em.

Shape a positive working environment, and you'll not only be better equipped to keep the good employees you have, you'll also be able to attract and hire even more good people. It's that simple.

Here are 80 ways you can improve retention and begin building *your* Magnetic Culture ...

1. **Stop, look, and listen!** Take this one to the bank: EVERY organization that has a Magnetic Culture **stops** every once in a while to assess their culture, **looks** at the information, and **listens** to what their customers, employees, and "stakeholders" are saying about the organization.

2. **Examine your written policies** to see if they reinforce or contradict your cultural objectives. For example: Do you state a belief in innovation, risk taking, and empowerment on one hand, yet have procedures that inhibit employee initiative with multi-level approvals required for routine decision making? If so, they have to change!

3. **Recognize the recognizers!** Want to send a message that you *really* believe in recognition for good performance? Do so by giving praise, performance rewards, and promotions to those who set the best recognition-giving examples.

4. **Examine your calendar ... and your "checkbook."** Nothing more dramatically indicates whether or not you truly support things like co-worker development, recognition, customer service, etc., than your calendar (how you spend your time) and your budget (how you spend your money). How you actually apply your resources is the true measure of your beliefs!

5. **Don't focus on info – focus on intelligence.** Hey, C.I.A. isn't short for Central *Information* Agency! The middle word is *Intelligence* ... and for good reason. The difference between information and intelligence is the data receiver's ability to *do* something (take positive action) rather than just *know* something. So, take business information sharing to the next level. Help people develop the ability to USE the data you provide.

6. **Deal with values violations!** Act as if your organization's values and operating principles are "page one" of your work rules. And treat those who violate these "rules" (trust, integrity, customer service, respect, etc.) with the same consequence they might face if they were caught stealing, for example. Fact is, when employees compromise your organization's values and principles, they ARE stealing – they're stealing your "cultural capital."

7. **Put THEM in the spotlight.** One of the best ways to GET credit is to GIVE credit to others. That way, everybody wins. And when everybody wins, most everybody *stays*.

8. **Create a self-assessing culture** by continually asking "How are we doing around here?" questions. And be sure you demonstrate to co-workers that giving and receiving constructive feedback about what's working well and what's not is a career *enhancing*, rather than a career limiting, activity!

9. **Encourage individual initiative.** Make sure people are rewarded for "walking the talk" and doing what needs to be done rather than pointing fingers, placing blame, and waiting for others to take the first step.

10. **Don't let performance appraisals get in the way of performance feedback!** Regardless of the effectiveness and frequency of your formal performance appraisal process, "people management" is an ongoing process of feedback, recognition, and coaching – with LOTS of opportunities occurring on a daily or weekly basis.

11. **Provide values-driven education.** Make sure that *everyone* gets specific training and skill building – not just your supervisors and managers. And be sure that all developmental activities include the tactical and practical "how-to" skills required to bring your mission and values to life!

12. **"Steady as it goes!"** Place emphasis on **lots** of small and consistent organizational improvements rather than a few big ones. And beware of "quick fixes," "programs of the year," and new "business religions."

13. **"We have to *start* meeting like this!"** Use *every* business meeting as an opportunity to reinforce your organization's cultural objectives. Meetings are a microcosm of the workplace – they're dramatic representations of principles like teamwork, empowerment, respect, etc.

> *"The cost of replacing an employee in today's market is roughly one half of that person's annual salary — a figure that doesn't include the loss of intellectual capital that results from each departure."*
> David L. Stum, Ph.D.
> The Loyalty Institute

14. **Celebrate heroes and "hero behaviors"!** One of the best ways to help people understand the importance of an issue is to give them clear examples. The behaviors you celebrate, and the individuals you recognize as "heroes," send a very clear and powerful message regarding expectations and criteria for success.

15. **Manage with "and's" rather than "or's."** Organizational goals can sometimes appear contradictory, such as: quality vs. productivity, profitability vs. integrity, and empowerment vs. consistency. The fact remains that these objectives aren't "or" issues. Rather, they're "and" considerations! They must be managed simultaneously – as equally important business objectives. The answer to "Which one do you want?" is **both!** Ongoing dialogue about this dilemma is one of the best ways to resolve perceived contradictions and develop understanding of different viewpoints.

16. **Remember that values *posted* must become values *practiced*!** Or, as a famous sports figure once said, "If you can't play it, don't say it!" And it's especially important to incorporate values education into new-employee orientation. Let people know, from day one, what's expected and what's important. Just be sure you don't preach principles in orientation only to have them quickly contradicted in the "real world."

17. **Develop a zero tolerance policy.** Don't allow yourself (or others) to make "special circumstance" exceptions to important principles and business ethics. Don't accept rationalizations like: "It was only a *small* indiscretion on the expense account," or "It was just a *little* joke about that religious group" (which is often justified because none of *them* work here). IT'S NEVER OKAY! So, don't allow these "small" exceptions to occur ... ever!

18. **Beware of "sheep-dip training"** – holding special education events designed to get rid of everyone's performance "bugs" and then sending everyone back to the same pasture. Department meetings, group discussions, and one-on-one coaching are often more effective vehicles for teaching co-workers the skills they need to build a high-performance organization.

19. **Stop blaming THEM.** You know, the "them" (whoever *they* might be – other than you, of course) that are causing the problem (whatever *that* might be). Rather than blaming "them," seek constructive solutions and encourage others to do the same.

20. **Check 'em first!** Whenever you make decisions – especially critical business decisions – make sure you check to ensure they align with the organization's values **before** they are implemented.

21. **Give new employees a history lesson.** Most organizations have great stories to tell about their origin, heritage, culture, and successes to date. People like to be a part of something or some place special. And telling stories is an excellent way to build that feeling.

22. **Take personal responsibility for communication!** Sure, the people at the top have a shared responsibility (operative word here is SHARED) to keep important information flowing, but so do you! The "acid test" of communication lies within the Golden Rule: Do unto others as you would have them do unto you. What information would *you* want or need to know? What would help *you* do your job more effectively and feel more involved or more engaged?

The more fair jobs you have,
the less job fairs you'll need!

–Steve Ventura

23. **Hire an outsider** ... a high-integrity professional with good business savvy to do a comprehensive review of your organization's formal policies and procedures. The task: To "test" them against your mission, vision, and values to see if they reinforce or contradict those cultural goals. You might be very surprised with the results of this exercise.

24. **Also, check to make sure your procedures are *timely*!** Periodically review your organization's policies, rules, and actual practices to ensure they make sense in today's "new world order" (i.e., global competition, technology advances, and the changing motivational requirements of new working generations).

25. **Don't dwell on *who* made the mess** ... just focus on cleaning it up! Fix things first – without looking for someone to blame – and get everyone's attention directed toward the future rather than focused on the past!

26. When you communicate with co-workers – formally or informally, by writing or speaking, strategically or tactically – **look for every opportunity to incorporate your organization's values**. Try it out. Take your next memo, e-mail, or meeting agenda and place it next to your values. See if your communication strategy reflects and reinforces those principles. If not, change it!

27. **Why ask why?** Because it's the best way to determine the reasons behind a person's beliefs, behaviors, and intentions! Good leaders ask lots of "why" questions of others ... and of themselves!

28. **Remember: People support what they help create!** This bit of common sense – right out of "Behavioral Science 101" – is still an important and underused principle. Everyone doesn't have to be in on *every* aspect of *every* decision, but people *do* need to contribute, at some level, to those decisions that affect their responsibilities. That is, of course, if you want to build co-worker commitment rather than just getting their compliance. You do, don't you?

29. **Develop "customer connections."** Get *everyone* directly involved with your customers in some fashion. Brainstorming will typically produce numerous low-cost ways to get everyone in your organization connected to your customer base. It will create greater meaning for your workforce ... and your customers will definitely appreciate it!

30. **Cultivate a recognition culture.** Even though truly effective recognition comes from the heart, tactical and practical techniques can be learned and taught to others. To make sure recognition becomes more than just a good intention, teach yourself and others the "how to's" as well as the "you oughta's."

31. **Wear clean underwear** as Mom suggested, "just in case!" Be sure that ALL the decisions and comments you make – including those made behind closed doors – pass the "clean underwear test" (a.k.a., If others could see or know what you're doing, what would they think?).

32. **Think USA!** When communicating with others, the objective goes beyond mere telling and hearing. The goal should be to build Understanding, Support, and Acceptance.

Chances are, the very best retention strategies already exist in your organization: your values and business philosophies.

Do you say you believe in concepts like quality, respect, customer service, trust, teamwork, diversity, and fair treatment?

Most organizations do! And the ones that retain the very best people are those that WALK THE TALK.

When it comes to facing the retention challenge, *let your values and operating principles be your guide.*

33. **Balance consistency with fairness.** There's no way to be perfectly consistent with all people in all situations – just like there's no way you can always be totally fair from everybody's perspective. But you can always include **both** considerations in your decision making to ensure that you have proper balance!

34. **Remember: Measurement matters!** Be sure that all formal (and informal) employee-assessment processes include values-driven practices such as integrity, responsibility, teamwork, etc., as well as bottom-line results. *Both* are important; therefore *both* need to be evaluated.

35. **Appoint a RETENTION CZAR (or CZARINA)** – a person with full- or part-time responsibility for being the central source of retention-based organizational resources. Just make sure this individual is not perceived as the ONLY person responsible for retention outcomes. In reality, each business unit manager has that ultimate responsibility. Can't afford a Retention Czar? Maybe you can't afford *not* to have one. Studies show that losing an employee costs organizations 50-200% of their average annual salary. And if your Czarina can stimulate a ten percent reduction in turnover ... well, *you* do the math!

36. **Survey people at ALL levels** to learn the collective attitudes about your organization's retention strengths and development opportunities. This will help identify trends, surface "hot spots," and give everyone a better picture of what, where, and how to change current attitudes, behaviors, systems, and practices.

37. **Give them the facts!** If you expect people to support significant organizational change, you have to give them the "straight scoop" on things like your organization's financial picture and the real impact of some new business competition. Only truly confidential information should be kept secret.

> The single best predictor of overall excellence is a company's ability to attract, motivate, and retain talented people.
>
> *Fortune* Magazine

38. *Don't* **carry a big stick!** Contrary to President Teddy's suggestion, the only big stick you ought to carry and use with your co-workers is the one that holds the BIG CARROT! That is, of course, if you hope to recruit and retain the best, brightest, and most productive employees.

39. **Don't be a "credit grabber"!** People who are guilty of this faux pas reduce their personal effectiveness and the effectiveness of their team. Instead of taking credit, leaders need to build the trust, commitment, and respect of their co-workers by *giving* credit for successes to "we" rather than to "me."

40. **Invest in education.** Devoting time and resources to developing people (and yourself) will provide significant and sustained bottom-line results. When you deal with many competing priorities, it's often easy to adopt a "we'll do it tomorrow" perspective. But as we all know, sometimes tomorrow never comes!

41. **Walk awhile in *their* shoes!** Spend some time – a week, a day, or even an hour – doing another person's job to get a first-hand perspective on the realities and challenges he or she faces. This will not only provide you with some significant insights, but also contribute to a culture of respect, collaboration, and business partnership.

42. **Do some "shameless bragging."** Add this recognition exercise to a future meeting agenda and give everyone a chance to brag on something positive in the workplace. Perhaps it's a great customer service success story, the accomplishment of a team goal, or the individual achievements of a co-worker. The point here is to get people focused on recognition, positive performance, and successes.

43. **Create CULTURE COPS!** Ask a few individuals to be watchdogs of the organization's culture. Although their job is to surface potential "values violations," their primary mission is to help build a high-performance organizational culture. Rotate this assignment to involve as many people as possible.

44. **Make an appointment to give recognition.** For example: Ask someone, "What's a good time tomorrow for me to give you some positive feedback?" This *let it simmer* strategy increases the recognition impact, gives the employee something to look forward to, and shows that you respect his or her time.

45. **Conduct a meeting *ON* your conference table!** To make a point with an individual or group, ask people to take off their shoes and stand on their chair (or table top) to enable everyone to see the "big picture" from that new vantage point. (Don't get carried away with this exercise, and be sure not to do anything dangerous.)

46. Turn training into "teachable moments." Suggest/ request/require all individuals attending development programs to share their learning experiences with co-workers. If precious organizational resources are allocated to an individual's personal and professional development, why shouldn't we ask them to multiply this investment by teaching others?

47. Establish an organizational "Who's Who" – an internal skills and expertise inventory for all to see and access. This inventory could include things like: Who in the organization knows about RFP's? Who has experiences with XYZ Enterprise, a potential new client? Who speaks fluent French? ... or any other set of skills and experiences that would be considered an organiza-tional asset.

48. Create a "Been There, Done That" intranet site – a place where all co-workers can post questions on a full range of technical subjects and tap the collective wisdom of the organization. Because there is basically no expense for such interchange, this technique has proven to produce an extremely high return on investment. And, it's another way of recognizing experienced performers.

49. Conduct a one-question survey on some regularly scheduled (quarterly, biannual, etc.) basis. Ask everyone in the organization to respond to the following (or a similar) open-ended question: "What can we do around here to help you be even more effective?" We're betting you'll be very surprised at the quantity and quality of the responses you receive.

50. Sponsor a "good news only day." This may be tough for some folks, but with practice and reinforcement, it's a great way to stay focused on the positive. It also fosters celebration of and learning from the practices, people, and perspectives that are contributing to the organization's success.

51. Develop a Cadre of Coaches. Create a group of highly respected "super coaches" – individuals with excellent people management skills. This is a way to give them specific recogni-tion and also provides an internal resource for the entire organi-zation.

52. Develop a "mystery customer program." Instead of hiring an outside company to test your organization's customer service attitudes and behaviors, use your own employees. The purpose is not to spy on specific individuals or departments, but rather to get everyone involved in understanding – and helping to improve – the organization's customer service culture.

53. Give people the freedom to make mistakes. An organi-zation's ability to attract the best and brightest people is often dir-ectly related to how management deals with mistakes that occur. Are they punished? Or, are they used as learning and development opportunities for individuals ... and the entire organization?

54. Let "warm body" employment candidates work some-where else! It can be tempting to fill a vacancy with someone who may have the required technical skills but a questionable attitude and behaviors. Do not (repeat: DO NOT) succumb to the temp-tation of adding this "warm body" to your team. You, your co-workers, and the organization's culture will be the ultimate losers.

55. **Talk less, listen more.** When coaching someone, you should talk no more than fifty percent of the time. Making it forty percent is even better! To ensure this happens, you need to prepare, rehearse, and maybe even do a practice coaching session with a colleague.

56. **Provide "on campus" personal services.** If you expect co-workers to give their all at work, then you need to make it easy for them to get some basic personal services at the workplace. Many service providers would be delighted to work with you and your organization to make such things as dry cleaning pickup and delivery, auto servicing, gourmet box lunches, etc., available at your workplace.

57. **When in doubt, throw them out!** Sorry for the harsh words here, but if a probationary employee is <u>already</u> creating attitude or performance uncertainties, you're better off cutting your losses early. Just be sure to coordinate with HR.

58. **Stop the Three C's: Contaminating** your **Culture** with **Complaining!** Hey, we all have disappointments and frustrations, but there's no need to spread your bad feelings to others. Doing so starts a spiral of negativity that solves nothing and stifles positive energy in the workplace.

59. **Be an environmentalist.** Pay close attention to your work "environment." For example: Are you trying to establish an atmosphere of teamwork and collaboration while you remain seated in the "power chair"? Look around. Your environment may be more *UN*conducive to your goals than you think!

60. **Be careful with secrets.** Forget that old saying: "What good is a secret if you can't tell someone?" Next time you plan to give a co-worker some "inside" or confidential information, think twice about it.

61. **"Extra! Extra! Read all about it!"** Assign everyone in the organization the responsibility of reading relevant trade journals, business magazines, newspapers, periodicals, etc. Then develop "pathways" to share the information learned with co-workers.

62. **Give *everyone* the chance to be a giver!** Many businesses today support charities and human service organizations. Consider enhancing these endeavors by allowing co-workers to directly participate. This might involve establishing a budgeted amount to be divided by the number of employees – with each donating to their charity of choice. It's a powerful way to reinforce teamwork and the spirit of giving. And it doesn't cost your organization any more than it's currently spending!

63. **Measure twice, cut once.** If you're going to make an important decision of any sort, "measure" the impact of that decision against the expected bottom-line results. And measure it again in terms of how it will be perceived by co-workers, your customers, and other organizational stakeholders. Then you can "cut" the decision!

64. **Make "enjoyment in the workplace" a recognized organizational value.** Ask co-workers for ideas on how this goal can be accomplished. People will appreciate that you've asked, and they'll routinely come up with practical, productive, and low-cost ways to create an enjoyable and high-performance workplace.

65. **Strive to create lessons** when others bring you problems. Solving the immediate problem may be your initial goal. But helping people develop the skills and confidence to independently handle similar issues in the future should be your second – and even more important – objective.

66. **Be an *active* listener!** Nothing sends a "you're important" message more than good listening. *Active* listening is more than just hearing ... it's getting involved in the conversation by asking questions, adding reinforcing comments, and letting the other person know you care about what they're saying.

67. **Play "red light, green light."** No, not the actual game from childhood, but an adult variation. In this version, green light time signifies those activities and efforts that make the organization GO and red light designates time wasters and things that STOP the organization from achieving success. The "game" is to find ways to minimize red-light events (e.g., fixing quality errors) and maximizing green-light activities (e.g., enhancing customer relationships).

68. This one bears repeating: **Test, test, and re-test your decisions** against your stated mission and values. The simple act of testing an important decision, by asking if it's in sync with your organizational principles, will produce both a healthy dialogue between co-workers and an outcome that is more likely to be aligned with your organization's operational philosophy and goals.

69. **Create awareness and understanding.** Make sure your organizational values, mission, vision, and operating principles are readily apparent, regularly communicated, and discussed frequently.

70. **Define your "killer applications"!** Identify the products and processes that make your organization or team special. Then find ways to concentrate even MORE energies and resources on them.

71. **Don't plant seeds in untilled soil!** Just as in nature, the seeds of organizational change need to be planted in "soil" that has been prepared to accept the germinating idea (by involving others) and has been fertilized with rich additives (information outlining the good business reasons for the decision).

72. *IN*spect what you *EX*pect! If you set an important plan or goal, give it the commensurate amount of follow-up, evaluation, measurement, accountability, and follow-through.

73. **Don't consider defensiveness offensive.** When dealing with hot issues that might involve significant differences of opinion, you may need to let an individual vent for a few moments. Emotional responses are often clues that can help you understand a person's state of mind and better deal with sensitive issues.

74. **Define, Assign, and Align!** Be sure you clearly **define** your mission, values, and goals. And **assign** everyone the responsibility of keeping organizational attitudes and behaviors **aligned** with these important objectives. If things get out of sync, celebrate the discovery and fix them. Then celebrate the fixing!

75. **Thin your herd of "sacred cows"!** Let's face it, some of the "ways we do things around here" (a.k.a. sacred cows) may have contributed to your successes to date, but they also may limit your success in the future! Occasionally, go on a "roundup" and thin the herd where necessary.

"Many companies define HR as being solely responsible for attraction, motivation, and retention.

Our approach has always been to entrust our great supervisors with that responsibility."

Elizabeth Barrett
V.P., Operations
The Container Store
(*Fortune's* "Best Place To Work" for two consecutive years)

76. **Watch your language!** No, this isn't about good manners. It's a reminder to use positive words and phrases in your communication, like: *Can do, We'll make it happen*, and *You can count on me*. These help create positive energy and positive expectations!

77. **Remember: Values management is like riding a bike.** When riding a bicycle, which is more important: pedaling, steering, watching for potholes, or being mindful of traffic? Fact is, they're all equally important! As in bicycle riding, it's a delicate exercise in balance with each organizational value being an important consideration in the journey to success.

78. **Be a Soul Man or Soul Woman** by actively involving and engaging the hearts and souls of your co-workers. There are literally thousands of specific tactics to make that happen, but it must begin with the leader understanding the importance of developing the organization's mind, body, and spirit!

79. **Provide freedom with fences.** Empowerment and participative decision making do NOT mean that everyone participates in all decisions equally! You do, however, need to provide high performers with a "large playing field" in which to exercise their creativity and initiative, and you need to clearly define their "fences" (i.e., boundaries, authority, timetables, budgets, etc.).

80. **Remember: You only have one chance to make a first impression.** Consider modifying your employee orientation process to help your new co-workers understand the culture of the organization as well as your policies, procedures, and protocols. For example, from day one, new employees should *feel* the importance of business ethics and customer service. Teaching new co-workers about your values and philosophies is just as important as giving them information about your retirement program!

RETENTION

SELECTION

ATTRACTION

To be the best and hire the best, you've got to ATTRACT the best

Building a Magnetic Culture also requires that you focus on **attraction** techniques. It's no secret that your number one concern is keeping the good employees you already have. But you also need to find additional qualified people who can fill openings resulting from growth, attrition, and some inevitable turnover.

Sure, the retention strategies in the previous chapter will help you create an environment that attracts good people. Some of the folks you're looking for will end up finding you! But there are many other things you can and should do to ensure a qualified candidate pool.

Here are 40 ways to help attract the best people and continue building *your* Magnetic Culture ...

-21-

81. **Use the "two click rule."** Make sure your organization's mission, vision, and values are no more than two mouse clicks from the front page of your website. Remember who may be browsing: customers, colleagues, and job candidates – lots of people important to the viability of your enterprise.

82. **Form a "values patrol."** Commission a task team to "seek and destroy" unnecessary organizational practices that are not contributing to your ability to recruit and retain the best and brightest people.

83. **Sponsor an open house** – an after-hours, well-promoted opportunity to welcome employees' families and friends. Use this event as a recruitment tool: Invite job applicants, placement professionals, teachers, and people from any organization that can help you attract good candidates. It's a great way to "win friends and influence people." (Thanks, Dale Carnegie!)

84. **Make new-hire orientation a recruitment strategy.** Yes, you've already attracted and selected these folks. But remember that they have friends and professional associates. How they're treated at every stage of employment – particularly, their initial experience with you – can influence their willingness to "market" your organization to others.

85. **Sell what they're looking for!** Expand your traditional recruitment strategies and job-posting methods to include information about your organization's climate, philosophy, and values – as well as personal and professional development opportunities.

86. **Establish a RAS Committee** – a permanent committee (with rotating members) that represents a functional and demographic cross-section of employees. The primary purpose of this task team is to make employee Recruitment, Attraction, and Selection (RAS) a core competency for your organization.

87. **Get rid of your best people!** Even though losing key individuals to advancement opportunities creates a temporary loss, the greater good is served by helping people learn, grow, develop, and reap the rewards accordingly. Losing their talents (the pain) will be offset by the organization's gain: The best, brightest, and most productive people beating a pathway to your door.

88. **Sponsor a food drive (or similar project).** You don't have to wait for some edict "from on high" to put together a meaningful community service project. You'll do something good for others, build departmental esprit de corps, and get great press and "PR" that can help to attract potential job candidates.

89. **Give *every* employee business cards.** What's the expense, a few dollars? For a small investment you enable employees to constantly be on the lookout for qualified candidates and use *their card* as an instant recruitment tool. Put your organization's mission and values on each card, plus information about your website.

90. **Consider job sharing.** Many top-notch people out there are looking for part-time work. Split a full-time job and you end up with one position and two great employees. And you may attract more who are looking for the same situation.

91. **Go where your applicants go** ... and don't be afraid to do some "out of box" thinking. One large housewares and furniture company saw a tremendous boost in applications when it started advertising in public restrooms. Think of the possibilities here!

Good people tend to attract other good people!

92. **Take a marketing approach to recruiting.** Go after potential employees just as proactively as you do new customers. Employment agencies always have available people because they're always recruiting. This ensures an adequate pool of candidates and helps to avoid desperation hiring.

93. **Remember: Job analysis and job description are two different animals!** A job description is written primarily for salary administration purposes, while a job analysis is for hiring. A job analysis includes things like capacity, attitudes, personality traits, interpersonal skills, etc. And, unless you're able to articulate these traits, you'll probably have difficulty attracting and selecting the right candidates.

94. **Set up a Retention Study Team** to benchmark other organizations, review exit interviews, and evaluate your retention "landscape." Use this team as a catalyst for removing retention obstacles and stimulating improvements. This will help create an environment that ATTRACTS good people.

95. **The best time to plant a tree is twenty years ago.** The next best time is today! Start NOW by scheduling at least one recruiting activity every day. You might call a colleague in a professional association and ask if they know any potential candidates. Or hire a summer intern, or start an employee referral program. The list of possibilities is endless.

96. **"Interview without end, Amen!"** This will help avoid the desperation-hiring syndrome, and it will allow you to build a pool of pre-qualified people that you can call upon when the need arises. Set a quota. A good rule of thumb is that for every new hire you need to conduct ten interviews. So, if you need three new people next year, you should conduct thirty interviews (or one every eight or nine days).

97. **Publicize community outreach programs.** An effective way to attract caring, concerned, and committed people is to let them know you have a caring, concerned, and committed organization.

98. **Remember: A good source for new employees may be the good folks that *used to* work for you!** Call your best *former* employees and see if they would like to come back. If not, ask if they know of anyone who might be interested in the job. Informal studies have found that approximately twenty percent of most management teams are composed of people who once left the employer and later came back.

99. **Another good source is all the good employees you now have!** New hires that are referred by current employees are more likely to be successful and stay on the job. Why? Because current employees tend to give candidates solid information about the job, and they typically have high standards for those they would like to have as colleagues.

100. **Recruit through vendors.** It's no secret that vendors are motivated to keep your business. And most would love to take credit for helping you land a great new hire. So keep reminding them that you are always looking for good candidates. Also, be sure to create some additional motivation with vendors by having your purchasing department help you with this strategy.

101. **Recruit through customers.** Put recruiting messages on sales receipts, in merchandise bags, on packaging, on product advertising, and of course, on your website. Everywhere and every way you communicate is potentially a good spot for a recruiting message.

102. **Recruit through employees' families and friends.** And, if you have an employee referral program, let them participate in it.

103. **Recruit through new hires.** On their first day, consider asking new employees: "Why did you leave your former employer? Why were you interested in our organization? Do you know anyone else that might be a good fit?" The answers to these and similar questions can provide some very usable information.

104. **Take a page from the U. S. Marine's "Buddy Program"!** Encourage friends to apply together. And if possible, tell them they will be able to work together ... or at the same location. Friends like working with friends.

105. **Recruit people with physical challenges.** Such individuals have proven to be extraordinarily capable, dependable, and highly motivated. And a number of federal and local government agencies train people with disabilities and integrate them into the workforce. You can start by calling the Job Accommodation Network at 1.800.526.7234 or visiting http://janweb.icdi.wvu.edu.

106. **Keep changing your recruiting message.** Different messages attract different types of people. The headlines that may attract good candidates for your sales force won't necessarily work for the accounting department or the loading dock. How can you tell which messages are working for what groups? Ask your newest and best employees what attracted them.

107. **Make *everyone* a recruiter.** This can include a host of possibilities ranging from participating in job fairs, to conducting focus group discussions, to soliciting ideas on how to attract and recruit the best and brightest talent available.

108. **Make your headline a grabber!** Phrases such as: "Invest in Yourself," "Starting Out or Starting Over?" and "Jumpstart Your Career!" can speak directly to the interest of a type of candidate you've described in the job analysis.

109. **Recruiting cards: Don't leave home without them!** Have your employees give them to people they meet at training seminars, as well as people who impress them at business and community functions. These cards should include contact information, a few lines about your organization, and perhaps something like: "We're always looking for valuable co-workers."

110. **Use Interns.** Internships are powerful ways to build relationships with potential candidates and their respective academic institutions. By making "every professor a recruiter," you're also likely to learn about qualified candidates way ahead of your competition.

111. **Make it easy to apply!** Chances are, most everyone you'd like to hire is already working. And working people don't have time to jump through a series of administrative "hoops" in order to get and submit an application – or to have their initial questions answered.

112. **The best way to make it easy is electronically!** People hate rejection ... which is why automated job hotlines, websites, and computer kiosks are successful in increasing the number of job applicants. These electronic systems eliminate the threat of personal rejection, are available "24/7," and in general, simplify the attraction and application process.

113. **"How did you hear about us? Why did you apply?"**
Ask these questions on your application, and study the responses
to identify which recruiting messages and tools worked the best.
Then increase your investment of time and resources where you're
getting good results and cut expenditures elsewhere.

114. **"Mystery shop" your recruitment process.** Using people
such as friends, co-workers, and colleagues in professional organizations, test your attraction and selection process "from soup to
nuts." The detailed feedback you receive will help you identify
what's working and what's not!

115. **Ditch the NOW HIRING sign!** When you really think
about it, "now hiring" isn't a reason for anyone to want to work
for you. Just like many of us learned in Marketing 101: Talk about
the features and benefits you have to offer. Communicate what's in
it for them. Try something like: "Interested in personal and professional development?" (or a similar approach).

116. **Don't insist on résumés up front.** Yes, eventually you
will need to collect this information. But a more viable first step in
attracting good candidates might be to ask them to apply by letter.
By doing so, you'll experience their communication skills and see
how they position their background, qualifications, and interest in
your organization.

Good hours, excellent pay, fun place
to work, paid training, mean boss. Oh
well, four out of five isn't bad.

Help Wanted ad, PA newspaper

117. "Ask me about a great place to work!" Give every employee a button bearing this slogan, and include it as a "tag line" on business cards. It encourages discussion about employment opportunities (people really *will* ask) and gets everyone helping with the recruitment challenge.

118. Have rules. Just don't have *dumb* rules! The recruitment game would be chaos without some ground rules. However, if you want to attract creative and innovative people, you can't burden your culture and strangle innovation with unnecessary red tape. Want to find out which "rules" people perceive as restrictive or outdated? Ask them!

119. Re-recruit your *current* employees! Don't give competing employers a chance to lure them away. Ask co-workers what they like best and least about their jobs, and then focus on expanding your organizational strengths and minimizing or eliminating the weaknesses based on the feedback you receive.

120. Market your culture. Make sure your recruiting message talks about important organizational characteristics such as learning and growth opportunities, flexible working hours, etc. Consider asking your best people what they like most about working in your organization and headline those benefits to attract more good people just like them.

Employees Aren't Assets After All

Most of the corporate mission statements painstakingly crafted in the 1990's included a version of the well-intended but overworked: *Our employees are our most important assets.* Now that the dwindling labor pool has all but evaporated and quality workers are increasingly hard to come by, the business community is beginning to realize that employees are not assets after all.

Companies do not own them, their market value doesn't show up on the balance sheet, and they cannot be sold or traded. What they are, in fact, are **investors**. They invest their time and talent for a promised return – be it just a paycheck or an opportunity to climb the corporate ladder. And, like investors, they can ride out the ups and downs of the marketplace for that return or they can bail out.

While there are hundreds of strategies you could use to reduce employee turnover, if you could do only two things, the most effective would be to set specific hiring standards and then treat employees like the investors they really are.

Where employees are viewed as *liabilities* – things that have to be controlled, regulated, and watched – turnover is rampant and has a stranglehold on growth and profits.

Thinking of employees as *assets* is a slightly more enlightened approach, but there exists the tendency to take assets for granted. When was the last time you appreciated a piece of equipment or your building? As with employees, you may have truly appreciated them when they were brand new, but now you just don't have time.

If you have investors, or have ever courted investors, take a moment to think about how you treat them, and compare that to how you interact with your employees. Any gap is an opportunity to improve employee retention ... and profits.

–Mel

selection

To
be the best
and attract
the best,
you've got to
HIRE
the best

It's no secret that Magnetic Cultures are made up of people. The better the people, the better the culture.

If done effectively, your efforts in the attraction arena (previous chapter) should produce an adequate and ongoing pool of employment candidates. It then becomes critical to have a **selection** process that identifies and brings on the cream of the crop.

Here are 60 ways to hire the best people and complete the circle of building *your* Magnetic Culture ...

121. HIRE TOUGH so you can MANAGE EASY! Too many managers rush through selection rather than taking the time and steps necessary to identify and hire the best person for the job. As a result, they have to spend an inordinate amount of time down the road fixing people problems. Take time in the beginning to do it right. As the old adage goes: You can pay in the beginning, or you can pay in the end ... with interest!

122. Draw a line in the dirt and stop hiring (and promoting) individuals who don't clearly demonstrate their beliefs and behaviors regarding values such as integrity, respect, responsibility, etc. Don't fall into the "belief trap" that you can train for these characteristics at some later date. It rarely happens!

123. Make every step in the hiring process a test. In addition to personality tests, skill tests, etc. (see #132), build in ways to "test" things like initiative, responsibility, and interpersonal skills. For example: Did the candidate review your website prior to the interview? Was the candidate courteous and friendly to members of your staff? The list of creative "test" possibilities is limitless.

124. Use applications for *everyone.* Applications are most important for the rights they protect ... yours. No matter how lofty the position, insist that everyone who interacts with your hiring system completes an application. (Coordinate with #111 and #116)

125. Hire people for who they are! The number one mistake most employers make is to value previous experience above all else. In today's rapidly changing world, however, experience is "how it used to be done" or "how we've always done it." Whenever possible, hire people for who they are – for traits like hard working, intelligent, good team players, etc. – rather than what they already know or have done before.

126. **Start with the five "kick-out" questions:** Does the applicant have the intelligence and physical capacities to do the job with or without accommodation? Does the compensation package meet the person's needs? Is the person willing to relocate if necessary? Can the person work the days and hours needed? Is the applicant willing to travel; does he or she have reliable transportation? If an applicant does not meet your minimum requirements, there is no sense in continuing the process.

127. **Keep an eye to the future.** Never take any hiring decision lightly. Who you hire today determines what your company will be like tomorrow.

128. **Pre-screen electronically.** A telephone or computer pre-screening step for basic capacities lowers the risk of liability and saves time.

129. **Mind your manners!** Whether applicants are good candidates or not, treat them with respect and courtesy. Thank them for applying. Tell them what they can expect in the hiring process. It's a very small world, and even if a person is not a good fit, he or she could be a potential customer or vendor.

130. **Use tools, not time.** Have applicants provide as much information on paper as possible. Your employment application, pre-employment testing, and reference verification forms are all tools that require the applicant's time, not yours.

131. No matter how hard new employees may be to recruit, **never "lower the bar."** The only difference between you and your competition is the quality of the people hired. Rigorous hiring standards are the fastest way to create a Magnetic Culture. Disney and Southwest Airlines are great examples: Candidates who *aren't* hired still speak highly of these organizations.

132. **Remember: To get the best, you have to TEST!** The most reliable predictor of success on the job is not experience, education, or age. The best predictor is testing. Test for every important criterion described in the job analysis.

> *Test for attitudes.* Simple, inexpensive tests can quickly screen for attitudes and traits that are most important (honesty, dependability, team orientation, etc.).
>
> *Test for personality.* If leadership, administrative, or supervisory skills are required, personality testing is the quickest and most reliable way to identify the best candidates. Not everyone is a "people person," and being brilliant doesn't necessarily make a person a good manager. Personality testing pinpoints each candidate's strengths and weaknesses.
>
> *Test for skills.* When skills are required (writing, presenting, driving, cooking, etc.), testing is the only way to be certain you will get what you need.

133. **Hire slow.** No matter how well you may know a person, put every candidate through the entire hiring process. People who complete this rigorous screening are proud of having been selected and bring that pride and commitment to work with them.

134. **Watch out for *too much* of a good thing!** If you're looking for a go-getter, make sure the person is not perceived as overly aggressive by others. If you are looking for someone with high attention to detail, make sure he or she is not so much of a perfectionist that the work never gets done.

135. **Establish a stakeholder selection team** – a cadre of trained internal and external people who are constantly looking to attract and "interview" (through informal conversations) high quality candidates.

136. **If you want to work with nice people, *hire* nice people!** Think about the behaviors you classify as "nice" or "desirable," and ask interview questions to see if the candidate routinely behaves that way. Examples: *Tell me about the last customer complaint you had to handle and what you did; Tell me about your relationship with a co-worker who was difficult in some way.*

137. **Hire for *tomorrow's* job.** Don't just hire for a position, hire for the future. Jobs, technologies, and markets are changing faster than ever. Hire people who are smart and adaptable.

> *The most expensive person you'll ever hire is the one you end up having to fire!*

138. **Remember: Better hiring decisions mean fewer management migraines.** Think about what all your best people have in common. It's likely they are optimistic self-starters who don't run to you with every little problem. It's usually the problem employees who take up the most management time.

139. **Hire people who are smarter than you!** They'll make you look great and help ensure the company's success. And as the adage goes: When you hire people smarter than you, you are smarter than them!

140. **Hire people who are different from you!** You don't need anyone else to think what you think and do what you do. You're already there! Look for fresh and different people who will bring fresh and different ideas. Hire for diversity.

141. Don't be fooled by age. Research proves that age is not a predictor of how well someone will do on the job. In fact, it has a negative predictive value of one percent. If you catch yourself thinking, "She's too old," or "He's too young," think again ... and stick to your job analysis.

142. *They've* **probably "read the book." Have you?** While many applicants are reading books and role-playing practice interviews, hiring managers are often left "winging it" with unstructured gut-instinct interviews. **Invest in employee selection and interview training** for every manager and supervisor involved in the hiring process.

143. Use "targeted" team interviews. Have multiple interviewers each focus on evaluating *different* applicant factors and characteristics. Divi-up things like work history, technical skills, teamwork, enthusiasm, honesty, and integrity amongst the group.

144. Duplicate your best. The use of testing will enable you to build a profile of what your best employees look like. Then you can hire to that standard in the future. Until you have this data base, use your best employees as your points of reference when writing up each job analysis.

145. Plan ahead. Before interviewing applicants who successfully make it through the application, pre-screening, and testing phases, go over all the paperwork and data collected. Plan your questions and arrange for a comfortable and uninterrupted setting.

146. "Hocus pocus, keep the focus!" To prevent applicants from derailing the interview, spell out your agenda clearly. Say something like: "First, I'm going to give you a brief overview of the job and our company. Then I'm going to ask you some questions. When I'm done, you'll have an opportunity to ask me any questions you might have."

147. Remember that *relaxed* people will tell you almost anything. Job interviews are stressful. Once you've explained your agenda, engage in a little small talk until you sense that the person is more relaxed. Ask about the traffic or the weather. Offer a soft drink or water.

POSITION APPLICANTS TO TELL YOU THE TRUTH

People show up for interviews primed to tell you only what they think you want to hear. Circumvent this by saying something like: *I'm going to be very open and truthful with you about the job and our company and I hope you're going to be open and honest with me about yourself. It doesn't matter if you've ever resigned, been fired, or had difficulty on a job. As long as you tell me about it, we can take it into consideration. But if you don't tell me, and we find out about it when we do our background check and look into your history, I can't hire you. Do you understand what it is I want?* Then wait for the applicant to respond before proceeding.

148. Try a "four question" interview:

First, to get an overview of an applicant's history, say something like: *Tell me about your very first paying job and three things you learned from it.* Most people will respond with some kind of part-time work during their school years. This gives you a glimpse into their work ethic and motivation. Then have the applicant tell you a little about each successive job and what was learned.

Second, for every trait, skill, or characteristic that is important to success on the job, say: *On a scale of one to ten, rank yourself in terms of* [e.g., communication skills] *and tell me your reasoning.*

Third, ask: *How were you rated for each of the areas we've just discussed on your last performance appraisal? Could you mail or fax me a copy of the last one you received?*

Fourth, ask: *Is there anything else you'd like to tell me about yourself and your abilities before I answer any questions you have?*

149. **Don't interview with the application or résumé in front of you.** If you do, you'll have a tendency to simply confirm the information you already have. The point of the interview is to gain further insight and understanding.

150. **Keep a "poker face."** Try to stay neutral in response to what you hear. If you look concerned or doubtful, the applicant will instinctively avoid providing any more information of that type. If you looked impressed, the candidate will keep giving you more of the same.

151. **Don't get lost in notes.** Maintain good eye contact and demonstrate interest as much as possible while making notes about those things that strike you as important. Do not, however, make a note about something negative while the applicant is speaking about it, as they may cut the response short and avoid disclosing anything else of a negative nature.

152. **Don't rate the applicant ... rate the applicant's *answers*.** If you conclude the interview feeling that you like the person and want to make an offer, go over your notes and pretend that a person you don't like gave you the same answers to a few questions. Are they still good answers?

153. **Pay attention to your "red flags"!**
Listen to what your intuition is trying to tell you. If anything the applicant does or says makes you uneasy, keep asking questions until you're certain you understand clearly.

154. **Ask "why" five times.** Psychologists say it takes five "why's" to uncover the real answer. To get to the bottom of an issue, tactfully continue asking "Why?" until you're satisfied.

155. **Remember: The body doesn't lie!** Research has found that about sixty percent of our intent is communicated not via words, but through body language. If you observe a change in body language from relaxed or poised to uneasy, say: "You seem uncomfortable about this," and wait for a response.

156. **Remember: You have two ears and one mouth for a reason!** The number one mistake interviewers make is talking too much. A good rule of thumb is that the applicant should do at least eighty percent of the talking.

157. **Listen for the "we" word ... unless you're looking for an "I" person.** One trait of good team players, be they managers or clerks, is the use of the word "we" when describing previous work situations and achievements.

158. **Ask everyone the same questions.** A structured interview composed of standardized questions asked of everyone is the best way to fairly evaluate applicants and avoid legal pitfalls.

159. **Use your Performance Appraisal Form in interviews.** Since selected candidates will be evaluated according to this form, use it to discuss applicant experience and success with the desired behaviors. For instance, if a part of your performance appraisal measures "ability to meet goals," ask what goals applicants have had and how they were met ... or why they weren't met.

160. **Ask *attitude* questions.** Examples of attitude questions are: "What is most important to you in a job?" "Tell me about a time you went out of your way to be honest." "What was your least favorite activity in your last job?" "What's your definition of a good employee?"

161. Ask *personality* **questions,** like: "Tell me about the last book you read." "How do you feel about meeting new people?" "Tell me about your most recent experience in a leadership position." "What do you criticize yourself for most often?"

162. Don't forget *skill* **questions.** Although you've tested for skills, use the interview to learn how and why the person acquired the skill, how long it took them to reach proficiency, and if they've ever taught the skill to anyone else.

163. Keep it legal! The last thing you need is a lawsuit. The easiest way to determine whether what you want to ask is discriminatory is to ask yourself if the question is directly related to the person's ability to do the job. Race, religion, national origin, marital status, age, disability, Workers' Compensation, and injury information  are all protected. Whether or not the person has children or dependents has no bearing on their ability to do the job. If your concern is dependability, ask: "How many times did you miss work this past year?"

164. Ask the *hard* **questions!** In addition to finding the best candidate for the position, it's also your responsibility to protect those already employed, your customers, and the organization's assets. Never assume that the clean-cut kid or well-dressed professional doesn't use drugs or has never committed a crime. Even if it's already on your application, during the interview, ask: "When was the last time you used illegal drugs?" "Have you ever been convicted of a felony?" It's much more difficult to lie or be evasive in person than on paper.

165. Be a buyer first and a seller second. If you are favorably inclined toward a candidate by the end of the interview, spend additional time selling him or her on both the job and the organization.

166. **Find out how to sell promising candidates on your job.** Ask, "What are your four major concerns about taking this job?" Then honestly address each concern.

167. **Close the interview on a positive note.** Whether you're favorably inclined or not, close by thanking the person for taking the time and being so forthcoming.

168. **Use an interview rating form**. From the job analysis, select the ten most important capacities, attitudes, personality traits, and/or skills that the ideal candidate for the job should possess. As soon as the interview is over, rate the candidate – based on his or her responses to questions in these areas – while the interview is still fresh in your mind.

169. **Ponder this: If gut feel is so good, why do so many new hires turn bad?** If your gut instinct says, *Don't hire this person*, DON'T! If it says, *Hire this person*, look for supporting evidence.

170. **Apply "the 30/30/30 rule."** While failing any one step in the hiring process rules a candidate out, never hire a person just because he or she *excelled* in one area. To make the best decision, weigh testing at 30 percent, the interview at 30 percent, and references at 30 percent. (Your personal perception or gut instinct weighs in for the final ten percent.)

171. **Take a candidate you're serious about to lunch** and observe their personal traits and behaviors. Things like table manners, conversation in an informal setting, and treatment of wait staff can be very revealing.

172. **Background checks: Don't hire without them.** When thousands of applications were screened by a reference/background checking service recently, it was found that one in ten applicants screened had a criminal record; one in three misrepresented themselves on the application; and one in four provided false education and credential records. If it's not already a part of your employment process, get written authorization from all applicants to check their references and run background checks.

173. **Use Reference Verification Forms.** These tools include the liability release waiver (signed by the applicant) and request basic information about each relevant former job and employer. The form is sent to the reference with a notation that you'll be calling. Make sure you document the contacts that you make – even for those who give you nothing more than basic employment verification.

174. **Make your selection process activities proportional to the job your filling.** A general rule of thumb: The more extensive the job responsibilities (CFO, department head, Hospital Administrator, Sales Director, etc.), the more rigorous the selection process.

175. **References: When all else fails, ask for a copy of the person's last performance review.** Then fax, write, or call to verify the information.

176. Whether you actually test for drugs or not, your recruitment advertising and materials can help **screen drug users out** if you include the statement: *Ours is a drug-free workplace.*

177. **Notify applicants who are not selected.** People who have made it through the interview have invested significant time and effort in pursuing a position with your organization. Thank them by phone and encourage them to try again.

178. **Don't automatically toss "the leftovers."** When you stick to your hiring standards, even your second and third picks may be excellent candidates. Ask yourself if you could place them in another spot in your organization. If not, let them know you'll be back in touch as soon as there's a suitable opening.

179. **Do a "post mortem"!** Each time you conclude your hiring activities, gather all involved staff and evaluate the process. How pleased are you with the overall outcome? What worked well? What didn't? What can you do to make the process just ten percent better the next time? Consider asking new hires for their input. And once you've collected this information, ACT ON IT!

Closing thought ...

180. **ENJOY THE ADDED BENEFIT!** The ideas presented in this handbook will help you find, get, and keep the best, brightest, and most productive people. And if you're successful at doing that, you'll experience a positive byproduct – an added benefit. The fact is, top-notch employees deliver top-notch customer service. And therein lies the true essence of a Magnetic Culture:

you attract and hold the employees you want AND the customers you need!

EMPLOYEES
you want

CUSTOMERS
you need

Check out these additional high-impact resources for ALL EMPLOYEES

Walk Awhile In *MY* Shoes – This revolutionary handbook helps you break down we v. they beliefs and behaviors that exist between "bosses" and "workers". OVER 1 MILLION COPIES IN PRINT! $9.95

Start Right...Stay Right – Every employee's straight-talk guide to personal responsibility and job success. Focusing on attitudes *and* behaviors, this best-seller is a *must read* for seasoned employees as well as new staff additions. $9.95

Leadership Courage – This hard hitting book surfaces some of the tough tasks and responsibilities of every leader, and gives the reader the techniques to be the best he/she can be! $14.95

VISIT WWW.WALKTHETALK.COM
for these and other WALK THE TALK® resources

The Authors

Eric Harvey is president of **The WALK THE TALK® Company** – the Dallas-based publishing and consulting firm that helps organizations adopt people practices that are in sync with their values and strategic objectives. His 30 years of professional experience are reflected in twenty-four acclaimed books, including the best-selling *Walk The Talk...And Get The Results You Want*; *Walk Awhile In MY Shoes*; and *The Leadership Secrets of Santa Claus*™

Mel Kleiman is managing partner of **The Hire Tough Group** – a division of Humetrics, Inc. – which provides employee recruiting, selection, and retention consulting services, workshops, presentations, and publications. Mel's popular books, *Hire Tough, Manage Easy*; *267 Proven Interview Questions*; and *Attract the Best, Repel the Rest* are available through his company's website and all major on-line booksellers.

Three easy ways to order
180 Ways To Build A Magnetic Culture

PHONE
Call **1.888.822.9255** toll free
or 972.243.8863
Customer Service Hours: 8:30 a.m. to 5 p.m. Central
Monday through Friday

WEBSITE
www.walkthetalk.com
Visit us on-line 24 hours a day

FAX
972.243.0815

Like your organization's name and logo to appear on books you buy? Ask us about "private labeling" for orders of 1,000+ books.

Call us today! 1.888.822.9255
or visit www.walkthetalk.com

Please send me extra copies of: *180 Ways To Build A Magnetic Culture*

1-99 copies $9.95 each   100-499 copies $8.95 each   500+ copies please call

180 Ways To Build A Magnetic Culture   _____ copies X   _____ = $ _____

Other WALK THE TALK Resources
Walk Awhile In *MY* Shoes   _____ copies X $9.95   = $ _____
Start Right...Stay Right   _____ copies X $9.95   = $ _____
Leadership Courage   _____ copies X $14.95   = $ _____

Product Total $ _____
*Shipping & Handling $ _____
Subtotal $ _____

Sales Tax:

(Sales & Use Tax Collected on TX & CA Customers Only)

Texas Sales Tax – 8.25% $ _____
CA Sales/Use Tax $ _____
Total (U.S. Dollars Only) $ _____

*Shipping and Handling Charges

No. of Books	1-4	5-9	10-24	25-49	50-99	100-199	200+
Total Shipping	$6.75	$10.95	$17.95	$26.95	$48.95	$84.95	$89.95+$0.25/book

Call 972.243.8863 for quote if outside continental U.S. Orders are shipped ground delivery 3-5 days. Next and 2nd business day delivery available – call 888.822.9255.

Name _____ Title _____

Organization _____

Shipping Address _____
        (No PO Boxes)
City _____ State _____ Zip _____

Phone _____ Fax _____

E-Mail _____

Charge Your Order: ☐ MasterCard   ☐ Visa   ☐ American Express

Credit Card Number _____ Exp. Date _____

☐ Check Enclosed (Payable to The WALK THE TALK Company)

☐ Please Invoice (**Orders over $250 ONLY**)   P.O. Number (required) _____

WALK THE TALK®

PHONE
1.888.822.9255
or 972.243.8863
M-F, 8:30-5:00 Cen.

FAX
972-243-0815

ON-LINE
www.walkthetalk.com

MAIL
WALK THE TALK Co.
2925 LBJ Fwy., #201
Dallas, TX 75234

Prices effective January 2006 are subject to change.